THE ENTREPRENEUR'S PLAYBOOK

HOW TO START, SCALE, AND SUCCEED IN BUSINESS

DAMI JOSH

Copyright © 2024 by DAMI JOSH

TABLE OF CONTENT

INTRODUCTION

Welcome to "The Entrepreneur's Playbook: How to Start, Scale, and Succeed in Business," a comprehensive guide designed to empower aspiring and seasoned entrepreneurs alike on their journey to success. In the dynamic landscape of business, navigating the intricacies of entrepreneurship requires a strategic approach and a wealth of knowledge. This book serves as your trusted companion, offering practical insights, proven strategies, and real-world examples to help you not only kick start your entrepreneurial venture but also thrive in the competitive business arena.

Drawing upon my years of experience and success as an entrepreneur, this playbook is crafted with a focus on actionable steps and invaluable lessons. Whether you're a budding business owner with a groundbreaking idea or a seasoned professional aiming to take your enterprise to new heights, this book is tailored to meet your needs. We'll explore the essential elements of entrepreneurship, from conceiving a viable business concept to executing effective scaling strategies.

"The Entrepreneur's Playbook" goes beyond traditional business guides by delving into the mindset and resilience required for success. In each chapter, you'll find practical exercises, case studies, and key takeaways that bridge the gap between theory and practice. From building a strong foundation to navigating challenges and capitalizing on opportunities, this playbook is a holistic resource that addresses the multifaceted aspects of entrepreneurship.

Prepare to embark on a transformative journey as we cover topics such as market research, financial management, effective leadership, and innovative marketing. Whether you're a solo entrepreneur or leading a team, this playbook equips you with the tools to make informed decisions, overcome obstacles, and turn your entrepreneurial dreams into a flourishing reality.

"The Entrepreneur's Playbook" is more than just a book; it's a roadmap to success, a mentor in print, and a companion for every stage of your entrepreneurial expedition. Let's turn your vision into a thriving business together.

CHAPTER 1: THE ENTREPRENEURIAL MINDSET

Welcome to the pivotal first chapter of "The Entrepreneur's Playbook," where we embark on a transformative exploration of "The Entrepreneurial Mindset." In the dynamic world of business, success is not solely defined by strategies, market trends, or financial acumen; it begins with the foundation of an entrepreneur's mindset. This chapter serves as a gateway to unlocking the potential within, cultivating the mental resilience, creativity, and adaptability essential for navigating the entrepreneurial landscape.

Here, we delve into the core principles that distinguish successful entrepreneurs—the ability to envision opportunities where others see challenges, the courage to embrace uncertainty, and the persistence to overcome setbacks. Understanding and embracing this mindset is the key to not only surviving but thriving in the ever-evolving world of business.

We'll explore the psychological aspects that underpin entrepreneurial success, addressing common challenges such as fear of failure, risk aversion, and the importance of maintaining a positive outlook. Through real-world examples, practical exercises, and insightful anecdotes, you'll gain a profound understanding of the mindset required to turn obstacles into opportunities and setbacks into stepping stones.

As we navigate this journey together, you'll discover how to foster creativity, cultivate resilience, and develop the adaptability needed to stay ahead in a rapidly changing business landscape. Whether you're a novice entrepreneur or a seasoned business leader seeking to enhance your mindset, this chapter lays the groundwork for the entire playbook, setting the stage for a successful entrepreneurial expedition. Get ready to embrace a mindset that not only fuels your ambitions but propels your business toward sustainable and impactful success.

- The mindset that fuels entrepreneurial success

The mindset that fuels entrepreneurial success is a dynamic and multifaceted aspect that goes beyond the conventional traits associated with business acumen. Successful entrepreneurs possess a unique mindset characterized by a combination of vision, resilience, adaptability, and a relentless pursuit of innovation. Here are key elements of the mindset that drive entrepreneurial success:

1. **Visionary Thinking:**

   Successful entrepreneurs have a knack for envisioning opportunities where others might see challenges. They possess the ability to think beyond the immediate circumstances and conceptualize a future that aligns with their goals and aspirations.

This visionary thinking enables them to set audacious goals and pursue ambitious ventures with unwavering determination.

2. Risk-Taking and Fear of Failure:

Embracing risk is inherent in the entrepreneurial mindset. Successful entrepreneurs understand that calculated risks are essential for growth and innovation. They are not paralyzed by the fear of failure but rather view failures as valuable learning experiences. This resilience allows them to bounce back from setbacks and approach challenges with a renewed sense of determination.

3. Adaptability and Flexibility:

The business landscape is dynamic, and successful entrepreneurs are adept at adapting to change. They embrace uncertainty and proactively adjust their strategies to navigate evolving markets and industry trends. This flexibility allows them to stay ahead of the curve and identify new opportunities that arise in a rapidly changing environment.

4. **Persistence and Resilience:**

Entrepreneurial success often involves overcoming numerous obstacles. A resilient mindset enables entrepreneurs to persevere through challenges, setbacks, and failures. This persistence is a driving force that keeps them focused on their goals even when faced with adversity.

5. **Continuous Learning and Curiosity:**

Successful entrepreneurs exhibit a lifelong commitment to learning and curiosity. They stay informed about industry trends, technological advancements, and emerging market opportunities. This thirst for knowledge enables them to make informed decisions, identify gaps in the market, and stay innovative in their approach.

6. **Positive Mindset:**

Maintaining a positive outlook is crucial for navigating the highs and lows of entrepreneurship. A positive mindset not only influences an entrepreneur's ability to handle stress but also fosters a collaborative and inspiring work environment. It attracts like-minded individuals and contributes to building a resilient organizational culture.

7. **Customer-Centric Focus:**

Successful entrepreneurs prioritize understanding and meeting the needs of their customers. They constantly seek feedback, listen to their target audience, and iterate their products or services accordingly. This customer-centric focus is instrumental in building a loyal customer base and ensuring long-term success.

In essence, the mindset that fuels entrepreneurial success is a unique blend of vision, resilience, adaptability, and a continuous pursuit of improvement. It is this mindset that propels entrepreneurs to not only weather the challenges of the business world but also to thrive and leave a lasting impact on their industries.

- Overcoming common mental hurdles and fostering resilience

Overcoming common mental hurdles and fostering resilience is a critical process in the entrepreneurial journey, as the challenges faced by entrepreneurs often extend beyond the realms of business strategy into the psychological and emotional aspects of leadership. Here's a breakdown of the process:

1. **Awareness and Acknowledgment:**

The first step in overcoming mental hurdles is recognizing and acknowledging their existence. Entrepreneurs must be introspective and identify specific challenges or mental blocks they face, whether it be fear of failure, self-doubt, or anxiety. Awareness is the foundation upon which resilience is built.

2. Cultivating a Growth Mindset:

Embracing a growth mindset is essential for resilience. This mindset sees challenges as opportunities for growth rather than insurmountable obstacles. Entrepreneurs with a growth mindset view setbacks as valuable learning experiences and understand that their abilities and intelligence can be developed through dedication and hard work.

3. Positive Self-Talk and Mindfulness:

Overcoming mental hurdles involves reshaping negative self-talk into positive affirmations. Entrepreneurs can cultivate mindfulness practices to stay present and focused, mitigating anxiety about the future or regrets about the past. Positive self-talk reinforces confidence and resilience during challenging times.

4. Learning from Failure:

Resilience is often forged in the crucible of failure. Entrepreneurs who can extract lessons from setbacks and view them as stepping stones rather than roadblocks are better equipped to navigate the uncertainties of business. Each failure becomes a source of valuable experience and a catalyst for improvement.

5. Building a Support System:

Entrepreneurship can be a lonely journey, and having a strong support system is crucial. This may include mentors, advisors, peers, or friends who can provide guidance, share experiences, and offer encouragement during tough times. Connecting with others who have faced similar challenges fosters a sense of community and resilience.

6. Setting Realistic Expectations:

Mental resilience is also about managing expectations. Entrepreneurs often face stress and burnout due to unrealistic expectations. Setting achievable goals, breaking down large tasks into smaller ones, and celebrating small victories contribute to a more sustainable and resilient approach to entrepreneurship.

7. **Adaptability and Flexibility:**

Resilience is closely tied to an entrepreneur's ability to adapt to change. The business landscape is dynamic, and mental flexibility allows entrepreneurs to pivot when necessary. Being open to new ideas, adjusting strategies, and embracing uncertainty are key components of overcoming mental hurdles.

8. Self-Care and Well-Being:

Prioritizing self-care is fundamental to maintaining mental health and resilience. Adequate sleep, regular exercise, and a balanced lifestyle contribute to emotional well-being. Entrepreneurs who prioritize their physical and mental health are better equipped to face challenges with clarity and resilience.

9. **Celebrate Progress, Not Just Success:**

Fostering resilience involves recognizing and celebrating progress, regardless of the scale.

Entrepreneurs should acknowledge the small wins, learn from the process, and appreciate the journey. This mindset shift reinforces a positive outlook and bolsters resilience in the face of ongoing challenges.

In conclusion, overcoming mental hurdles and fostering resilience is an ongoing, intentional process that requires self-awareness, a growth mindset, and a commitment to well-being. By navigating challenges with a positive and adaptable mindset, entrepreneurs can not only overcome obstacles but also thrive in the ever-evolving landscape of business.

- Cultivating creativity and adaptability for sustainable growth

Cultivating creativity and adaptability is essential for entrepreneurs seeking sustainable growth in today's dynamic business environment. This process involves fostering a culture of innovation, encouraging out-of-the-box thinking, and adapting strategies to meet evolving market demands. Here's a breakdown of the key steps in cultivating creativity and adaptability for sustainable growth:

1. Encourage a Culture of Innovation:

Create an organizational culture that values and encourages innovation. This involves fostering an environment where employees feel empowered to share ideas without fear of judgment. Establish channels for open communication and idea-sharing, and recognize and reward innovative thinking.

2. Diversity and Inclusion:

Embrace diversity in your team. A diverse workforce brings together individuals with different perspectives, experiences, and problem-solving approaches. This diversity fuels creativity by introducing a range of ideas and insights, fostering a more adaptable and innovative organization.

3. Provide Learning Opportunities:

Continuous learning is crucial for cultivating creativity and adaptability. Invest in training programs, workshops, and educational opportunities for your team to stay updated on industry trends, new technologies, and emerging market dynamics. This learning culture enhances adaptability and fuels creative thinking.

4. Cross-Functional Collaboration:

Break down silos within your organization and encourage collaboration between different departments. Cross-functional teams bring together diverse skills and expertise, fostering creativity and adaptability as team members learn from each other and approach challenges from multiple perspectives.

5. Embrace Failure as a Learning Opportunity:

Create a culture where failure is not stigmatized but seen as a stepping stone to success. Encourage experimentation and risk-taking, emphasizing the importance of learning from failures. This mindset shift promotes adaptability by instilling resilience and a willingness to iterate on ideas.

6. Allocate Time for Creative Thinking:

Dedicate specific time for creative thinking and brainstorming sessions. Whether through regular team meetings or designated innovation days, allowing time for unstructured thinking can spark creative ideas and solutions. This intentional focus on creativity contributes to adaptability in the long run.

7. Stay Customer-Centric:

Cultivating creativity involves understanding and meeting the needs of your customers. Regularly solicit feedback, conduct market research, and stay attuned to changing customer preferences. Being customer-centric ensures that your products or services remain relevant and adaptable to evolving market demands.

8. Adopt Agile Practices:

Embrace agile methodologies in project management. Agile practices promote adaptability by breaking down projects into manageable iterations, allowing for continuous feedback and adjustments. This iterative approach enables organizations to respond swiftly to changes in the market or customer needs.

9. Encourage Entrepreneurial Thinking:

Foster an entrepreneurial mindset within your organization. Encourage employees to think like entrepreneurs, take ownership of their projects, experiment with new ideas, and embrace a proactive approach to problem-solving. This mindset fosters both creativity and adaptability.

10. Leadership Support and Modeling:

Leadership plays a crucial role in fostering a culture of creativity and adaptability. Leaders should actively support and model these traits, demonstrating a willingness to embrace change, encouraging innovative thinking, and celebrating adaptability as a core competency.

In summary, cultivating creativity and adaptability for sustainable growth is a multifaceted process that involves nurturing a culture of innovation, promoting continuous learning, embracing diversity, and encouraging a customer-centric approach. By instilling these principles into the fabric of your organization, you create a foundation for sustained success in an ever-evolving business landscape.

CHAPTER 2: FROM IDEA TO BUSINESS PLAN

Welcome to the pivotal chapter in "The Entrepreneur's Playbook" where we embark on the transformative journey "From Idea to Business Plan." In the dynamic realm of entrepreneurship, the spark of an idea is just the beginning—its realization and success hinge on the meticulous crafting of a comprehensive business plan. This chapter serves as a guiding compass for aspiring and seasoned entrepreneurs alike, navigating the crucial steps that bridge the gap between a visionary concept and a strategically outlined roadmap for business success.

Here, we dive into the essential process of transforming creative inspiration into a tangible and executable plan. Whether you're in the nascent stages of brainstorming your venture or seeking to refine an existing idea, the insights within this chapter will empower you to articulate your vision with clarity, define your objectives with precision, and establish a solid foundation for the journey ahead.

We'll explore the art of conducting thorough market research, understanding your target audience, and refining your value proposition. Through practical exercises and real-world examples, you'll gain the tools to identify opportunities, assess potential challenges, and articulate a compelling narrative that not only captivates stakeholders but also serves as a blueprint for your entrepreneurial venture.

Crafting a business plan is more than a mere formality—it is a dynamic process that compels entrepreneurs to critically analyze every facet of their idea. It is a roadmap that aligns aspirations with actionable strategies, providing a framework for decision-making, resource allocation, and long-term sustainability.

As we navigate "From Idea to Business Plan" together, envision this chapter as your dedicated guide, offering insights, templates, and best practices to transform the intangible into the tangible. Your entrepreneurial journey is about gaining structure and purpose, setting the stage for a successful business venture built on a solid foundation of strategic planning and vision. Let's dive into the heart of entrepreneurship, where ideas take shape and dreams become reality.

- Nurturing innovative business concepts

Nurturing innovative business concepts is a crucial aspect of the entrepreneurial journey, as it lays the foundation for creating unique and viable solutions that meet market needs. The process involves fostering creativity, encouraging idea generation, and systematically refining concepts to bring them to fruition. Here's a comprehensive breakdown of the steps involved in nurturing innovative business concepts:

1. Cultivate a Creative Culture:

Establish an organizational culture that values and promotes creativity. Encourage an open exchange of ideas, reward innovative thinking, and create an environment where team members feel empowered to explore unconventional solutions. A culture that nurtures creativity is essential for fostering innovative business concepts.

2. Identify Market Needs and Opportunities:

Begin by conducting thorough market research to identify gaps, challenges, and opportunities. Understanding the needs of your target audience and the competitive landscape provides a foundation for generating innovative business concepts that address specific pain points or offer unique value propositions.

3. **Encourage Cross-Functional Collaboration:**

Foster collaboration between individuals with diverse skills and backgrounds. Cross-functional teams bring different perspectives to the table, sparking creativity and facilitating the generation of innovative ideas. Collaborative efforts often result in comprehensive and well-rounded business concepts.

4. **Regular Idea Generation Sessions:**

Schedule regular brainstorming sessions to generate a continuous flow of ideas. These sessions can be structured or unstructured, involving team members from various departments. Encourage the free exchange of thoughts and the exploration of wild and unconventional ideas without immediate judgment.

5. **Embrace Failure as a Part of Innovation:**

Create a culture that views failure not as a setback but as a stepping stone to success. Innovation often involves experimentation, and not all ideas will succeed on the first attempt. Encouraging a mindset that embraces failure as a learning opportunity fosters resilience and perseverance in the face of challenges.

6. Use Design Thinking Principles:

Apply design thinking principles to the ideation process. This human-centered approach involves empathizing with users, defining problems, ideating solutions, prototyping, and testing. Design thinking encourages iterative problem-solving and ensures that innovative concepts are user-centric and practical.

7. Seek External Perspectives:

Engage with external stakeholders, industry experts, and potential customers to gain diverse perspectives on your business concepts. External input can provide valuable insights, identify blind spots, and help refine ideas based on real-world feedback.

8. **Prioritize Scalability and Sustainability:**

Assess the scalability and sustainability of your innovative business concepts. Consider long-term viability, potential for growth, and environmental impact. Sustainable innovation not only addresses current needs but also anticipates future trends and challenges.

9. **Create a Prototype or Minimum Viable Product (MVP):**

Develop a prototype or MVP to test the feasibility of your innovative concept in a real-world setting. Prototyping allows you to gather user feedback, identify potential improvements, and make data-driven decisions before fully implementing the concept.

10. **Iterate and Refine:**

Embrace a continuous improvement mindset. Based on feedback, data, and evolving market conditions, iterate and refine your innovative business concepts. The ability to adapt and refine ideas over time is crucial for staying relevant and competitive.

11. **Protect Intellectual Property:**

If your innovative concept involves unique intellectual property, consider seeking legal protection through patents, trademarks, or copyrights. Protecting your intellectual property is essential for maintaining a competitive edge in the market.

12. **Communicate Effectively:**

Clearly articulate the value proposition of your innovative business concepts. Effective communication is key when presenting your ideas to stakeholders, investors, or potential collaborators. A compelling narrative enhances the likelihood of gaining support and resources for implementation.

By systematically following these steps, entrepreneurs can create an environment conducive to innovative thinking, generate unique business concepts, and position themselves for success in a rapidly evolving business landscape. Nurturing innovation is an ongoing process that requires adaptability, creativity, and a commitment to pushing the boundaries of what is possible.

- Conducting effective market research

Conducting effective market research is a foundational step in the entrepreneurial journey, providing valuable insights that inform strategic decision-making and increase the likelihood of business success. Here's a comprehensive breakdown of the process:

1. **Define Objectives and Research Questions:**

Clearly outline the objectives of your market research. Whether you're entering a new market or refining an existing product, establish specific research questions that guide your investigation.

This clarity ensures focused and relevant data collection.

2. Identify Target Audience:

Define your target audience or customer segment. Understanding the demographics, behaviors, and preferences of your potential customers helps tailor the research to gather insights that directly impact your business.

3. Choose Research Methods:

Select appropriate research methods based on your objectives. Common methods include surveys, interviews, focus groups, observations, and data analysis. A combination of quantitative and qualitative approaches often provides a comprehensive understanding of the market.

4. Develop a Research Plan:

Create a detailed research plan outlining the scope, timeline, and budget for your market research. Clearly define roles and responsibilities, and establish protocols for data collection, analysis, and reporting.

5. **Collect Secondary Data:**

Start by gathering existing data from secondary sources, such as industry reports, academic publications, government publications, and competitor analyses. Secondary data provides a foundational understanding of the market landscape.

6. **Conduct Primary Research:**

Implement primary research methods to collect firsthand data tailored to your specific needs. Surveys and interviews are effective for understanding customer preferences, while focus groups provide insights into attitudes and perceptions.

7. **Survey Design:**

If using surveys, design clear, concise, and unbiased questionnaires. Ensure questions are structured to gather actionable data and consider using a mix of closed-ended and open-ended questions to capture both quantitative and qualitative insights.

8. Interview and Focus Group Moderation:

If conducting interviews or focus groups, carefully moderate sessions to encourage open and honest responses. Use probing questions to delve deeper into participants' thoughts and experiences.

9. Analyze Data:

Systematically analyze the collected data. Use statistical tools for quantitative data and thematic analysis for qualitative data. Identify patterns, trends, and correlations that offer meaningful insights into market dynamics.

10. Interpret Findings:

Interpret the research findings in the context of your business objectives. Identify key takeaways, opportunities, and potential challenges. Consider how the research aligns with your overall business strategy.

11. Competitor Analysis:

Evaluate competitors within the market. Understand their strengths, weaknesses, market share, and customer perceptions. This analysis provides a benchmark for positioning your business and uncovering potential differentiation strategies.

12. SWOT Analysis:

Conduct a SWOT analysis (Strengths, Weaknesses, Opportunities, and Threats) based on the collected data. This strategic analysis helps identify internal and external factors that can influence your business strategy.

13. Validate and Refine:

Validate your findings through additional research or by seeking feedback from industry experts, mentors, or potential customers. Use this feedback to refine your market research and ensure its accuracy and relevance.

14. **Compile and Present Results:**

Compile your research findings into a comprehensive report. Present key insights, supported by data and visualizations. Communicate the implications for your business strategy and decision-making.

15. **Implement Insights:**

Translate research insights into actionable strategies. Whether adjusting your marketing approach, refining product features, or entering a new market segment, use the research to inform and guide your business decisions.

Conducting effective market research is an iterative process that requires continuous refinement based on evolving market dynamics. By investing time and resources into thorough research, entrepreneurs can make informed decisions that align with market needs and increase the likelihood of business success.

- Crafting a comprehensive and compelling business plan

Crafting a comprehensive and compelling business plan is a critical step in the entrepreneurial journey, serving as a roadmap that outlines your business goals, strategies, and operational details. Here's a detailed breakdown of the process:

1. **Executive Summary:**

   - Concisely summarize your business idea, mission, vision, and the problem you aim to solve.

   - Highlight key aspects, such as target market, unique value proposition, and financial projections.

2. **Business Description:**

- Provide a detailed overview of your business, including its legal structure, location, and history.

- Explain the mission, vision, and values that guide your company.

3. Market Analysis:

- Conduct a thorough analysis of your target market, including size, demographics, trends, and growth potential.

- Assess your competitors and perform a SWOT analysis (Strengths, Weaknesses, Opportunities, and Threats).

4. Organization and Management:

- Outline your business's organizational structure, including key team members, their roles, and expertise.

- Provide resumes or bios for key team members, emphasizing relevant experience.

5. Product or Service Offering:

- Clearly describe the products or services you offer, emphasizing their unique features and benefits.

- Highlight any intellectual property, proprietary technology, or competitive advantages.

6. **Marketing and Sales Strategy:**

- Detail your marketing and sales approach, including target customer segments, channels, and pricing strategy.

- Present your promotional activities, advertising plans, and sales forecasts.

7. **Funding Request (if applicable):**

- If seeking funding, clearly specify the amount, purpose, and terms of the funding request.

- Provide a breakdown of how the funds will be utilized and the expected return on investment.

8. **Financial Projections:**

- Present detailed financial forecasts, including income statements, balance sheets, and cash flow statements.

- Include projections for the next three to five years, demonstrating a clear understanding of your business's financial health.

9. Risk Analysis:

- Identify potential risks and challenges your business may face.

- Develop strategies for mitigating these risks and reassure investors or stakeholders about your risk management approach.

10. Implementation Plan:

- Outline the step-by-step plan for implementing your business idea.

- Include key milestones, timelines, and responsibilities to demonstrate a clear path for execution.

11. **Monitoring and Measurement:**

- Describe how you will monitor and measure the success of your business.

- Identify key performance indicators (KPIs) and milestones to track progress.

12. **Appendix:**

- Include any supporting documents, such as market research data, resumes of key team members, or additional financial information.

- Use this section to provide supplementary details that enhance the credibility of your plan.

13. **Formatting and Presentation:**

- Ensure your business plan is professionally formatted, with clear headings, charts, and visuals.

- Tailor the presentation style to your audience, whether it's investors, lenders, or internal stakeholders.

14. Seek Feedback:

- Before finalizing your business plan, seek feedback from mentors, advisors, or industry experts.

- Incorporate constructive feedback to strengthen the overall quality and persuasiveness of your plan.

15. Regular Updates:

- Treat your business plan as a living document that evolves with your business.

- Regularly update your plan to reflect changes in the market, business strategy, or financial projections.

Crafting a comprehensive and compelling business plan requires a balance of creativity, strategic thinking, and attention to detail. By following this structured process, entrepreneurs can articulate their vision, demonstrate viability, and attract the support needed to turn their business ideas into successful ventures.

CHAPTER 3: BUILDING THE FOUNDATION

Welcome to the pivotal chapter of "The Entrepreneur's Playbook" where we embark on the transformative journey of "Building the Foundation." In the intricate tapestry of entrepreneurship, success is intrinsically tied to the strength and resilience of the foundation upon which your venture stands. This chapter serves as your guide to the fundamental elements that lay the groundwork for a thriving business—from establishing a robust legal framework to assembling a dynamic team and fostering a culture that propels innovation and growth.

Here, we delve into the critical building blocks that form the core infrastructure of your enterprise. Whether you are at the inception of your entrepreneurial voyage or looking to fortify an existing business, the insights within this chapter are crafted to empower you with the tools and knowledge needed to construct a solid foundation that withstands the tests of time and industry evolution.

We'll explore the legal considerations essential for safeguarding your business, the intricacies of choosing the right organizational structure, and the pivotal role of assembling a talented and motivated team. Additionally, we'll delve into the intangible yet powerful components of building a strong company culture that fosters innovation, adaptability, and a collective sense of purpose.

Consider this chapter as your architectural blueprint, guiding you through the construction of a foundation that not only sustains your business but also serves as a Launchpad for ambitious growth and enduring success. As we navigate the process of "Building the Foundation" together, envision the creation of a resilient and dynamic groundwork that propels your entrepreneurial aspirations to new heights. Get ready to lay the cornerstone of your success and embark on a journey that transforms your vision into a thriving reality.

- Legal considerations and business structure

Legal considerations and choosing the right business structure are foundational elements in the process of establishing a robust and sustainable business foundation. These decisions have far-reaching implications for the operational, financial, and legal aspects of an enterprise. Let's delve into the key aspects of legal considerations and business structure:

Legal Considerations:

1. Business Registration and Compliance:

  - **Legal Structure:** Choose a legal structure for your business, such as a sole proprietorship, partnership, limited liability company (LLC), or corporation. Each structure has different implications for liability, taxation, and governance.

- **Business Name:** Register a unique and legally compliant business name to distinguish your entity in the market.

2. Intellectual Property Protection:

- **Trademarks and Patents:** Identify and protect your intellectual property, including trademarks for branding and patents for unique inventions. This safeguards your innovations from unauthorized use by competitors.

3. Contracts and Agreements:

- **Client Contracts:** Draft comprehensive contracts outlining terms of service, payment terms, and deliverables to protect both your business and clients.

- **Employee Agreements:** Establish clear employment contracts that outline roles, responsibilities, compensation, and any non-disclosure or non-compete agreements.

4. Regulatory Compliance:

- **Industry Regulations:** Understand and comply with industry-specific regulations and standards applicable to your business.

- **Licenses and Permits:** Obtain necessary licenses and permits to operate legally in your jurisdiction.

5. Data Protection and Privacy:

- **Privacy Policies:** Develop and implement privacy policies to protect customer data and comply with data protection regulations.

- **Data Security Measures:** Implement robust data security measures to safeguard sensitive information.

Business Structure:

1. Sole Proprietorship:

- **Ownership:** Owned and operated by a single individual.

- **Liability:** The owner is personally liable for business debts and obligations.

- **Taxation:** Business income is reported on the owner's tax return.

2. **Partnership:**

- **Ownership:** Jointly owned by two or more individuals.

- **Liability:** Partners share liability for business debts.

- **Taxation:** Profits and losses are passed through to individual partners' tax returns.

3. **Limited Liability Company (LLC):**

- **Ownership:** Members own the LLC.

- **Liability:** Members' assets are protected from business debts.

- Taxation: Can choose to be taxed as a pass-through entity or a corporation.

4. Corporation:

- **Ownership:** Owned by shareholders.

- **Liability:** Shareholders' assets are generally protected.

- **Taxation:** Subject to corporate taxation, and dividends are taxed at the individual level.

5. S Corporation:

- **Ownership:** Similar to a regular corporation but with restrictions on the number and types of shareholders.

- **Liability:** Shareholders' assets are generally protected.

- **Taxation:** Profits and losses pass through to individual shareholders' tax returns.

Considerations for Choosing a Business Structure:

- **Liability Protection:** Assess the level of personal liability protection you need for your business.

- **Tax Implications:** Consider the tax implications of each structure and choose the one that aligns with your financial goals.

- **Ownership and Management Structure:** Evaluate how you want to structure ownership and management within your business.

- **Flexibility and Complexity:** Consider the administrative and regulatory requirements associated with each structure.

In conclusion, the legal considerations and choice of business structure are integral to the foundational aspects of entrepreneurship. Seeking legal advice and carefully evaluating the specific needs and goals of your business will contribute to a solid foundation, positioning your enterprise for legal compliance, operational efficiency, and long-term success.

- Assembling a winning team

Assembling a winning team is a critical component of building a successful business. The synergy and collective capabilities of the team can significantly impact the company's culture, innovation, and overall performance. Here's a comprehensive guide to the process of assembling a winning team:

1. **Define Your Team Needs:**

- Identify Roles and Responsibilities:

Clearly define the roles and responsibilities required for your business. Understand the skills, expertise, and characteristics needed for each position.

- Cultural Fit:

Consider the cultural aspects of your team. Define the values, work ethic, and communication styles that align with your company culture.

2. Develop a Recruitment Strategy:

- Craft a Compelling Job Description:

Clearly articulate the expectations, qualifications, and benefits associated with each role in your job descriptions. Highlight the unique aspects of your company culture.

- Utilize Various Channels:

Use a mix of recruitment channels, including online job boards, social media, networking events, and industry-specific platforms, to reach a diverse pool of candidates.

- Leverage Employee Referrals:

Encourage current team members to refer potential candidates. Employee referrals often result in hires who fit well within the existing team and culture.

3. Implement a Rigorous Hiring Process:

- Screen Resumes and Applications:

Review resumes and applications to shortlist candidates who meet the basic qualifications and skills outlined in the job description.

- Conduct Initial Interviews:

Conduct initial interviews to assess candidates' communication skills, cultural fit, and enthusiasm for the role and company.

- Skills Assessment and Testing:

Administer skills assessments or tests relevant to the job to evaluate candidates' abilities and competencies.

- Behavioral Interviews:

Conduct behavioral interviews to understand how candidates approach problem-solving, handle challenges, and collaborate with others.

4. Prioritize Soft Skills:

- Communication Skills:

Prioritize candidates with strong communication skills, both verbal and written, as effective communication is vital for teamwork.

- Adaptability:

Look for candidates who demonstrate adaptability and a willingness to learn. The ability to adapt to changing circumstances is crucial for a dynamic work environment.

- Collaboration and Teamwork:

Assess candidates' experience in and attitude toward collaboration. Winning teams thrive on effective teamwork and mutual support.

5. Evaluate Cultural Fit:

- Company Values Alignment:

Ensure that candidates share and align with the core values and mission of your company. A strong cultural fit enhances team cohesion.

- Team Dynamics:

Consider how the candidate's personality and working style will complement the existing team dynamics.

6. Offer Competitive Compensation and Benefits:

- Competitive Salary:

Provide a competitive salary that reflects the industry standards and the candidate's experience and qualifications.

- Benefits and Perks:

Offer attractive benefits and perks, such as health insurance, retirement plans, flexible working arrangements, and professional development opportunities.

7. Onboarding and Integration:

- Structured Onboarding Program:

Develop a structured onboarding program to integrate new team members seamlessly into the organization. Provide necessary training and orientation.

- Mentorship and Support:

Assign mentors or buddies to new team members to provide guidance, and support, and help them acclimate to the company culture.

8. Foster a Positive Work Environment:

- Encourage Open Communication:

Cultivate an environment where open communication is encouraged, and team members feel comfortable expressing ideas and concerns.

- Recognition and Rewards:

Implement a system for recognizing and rewarding achievements. Acknowledging individual and team accomplishments contributes to morale and motivation.

9. Continuous Learning and Development:

- Invest in Training:

Provide opportunities for continuous learning and professional development to help team members stay updated on industry trends and technologies.

- Performance Reviews:

Conduct regular performance reviews to provide constructive feedback and identify areas for improvement and growth.

10. **Monitor Team Dynamics:**

- Team Building Activities:

Organize team-building activities and events to strengthen relationships and enhance team cohesion.

- Address Conflicts Promptly:

Address conflicts or issues within the team promptly and constructively. A healthy team dynamic requires open communication and conflict resolution.

By following these steps, you can systematically build a winning team that not only possesses the necessary skills but also aligns with your company's values, fosters innovation, and contributes to the overall success of your business.

- Establishing a strong company culture and values

Establishing a strong company culture and values is a fundamental aspect of building a cohesive and successful organization. A positive and well-defined culture contributes to employee engagement, attracts top talent, and shapes the identity of the company. Here's a comprehensive guide to the process of establishing a strong company culture and values:

1. **Define Core Values:**

- Leadership Input:

Involve leaders and key stakeholders in defining the core values. Leadership input is crucial for aligning values with the overall vision and mission of the company.

- Employee Involvement:

Encourage input from employees at various levels. This inclusivity ensures that the values resonate with the entire workforce and reflect diverse perspectives.

- Identify Aspirational Values:

Aspirational values should represent the ideal behaviors and principles that the company strives to embody. These values set a standard for the desired company culture.

2. Communicate Values Clearly:

- Craft a Values Statement:

Develop a clear and concise values statement that articulates the core principles guiding the company. This statement should be easily understandable and memorable.

- Integration into Branding:

Integrate the values into the company's branding, internal communications, and external messaging. Reinforce the values through visual elements, such as logos, and consistently communicate them across various platforms.

3. **Lead by Example:**

- Leadership Demonstration:

Leadership should embody the values in their actions and decisions. When leaders consistently demonstrate their values, it sets the tone for the entire organization.

- Highlight Positive Behaviors:

Acknowledge and celebrate instances where employees exemplify the company values. Recognize and reward positive behaviors that align with the established culture.

4. **Integrate Values into Work Practices:**

- **Recruitment and Onboarding:**

Incorporate values into the recruitment process to attract candidates who align with the company culture. During onboarding, emphasize the importance of these values in daily work.

- **Performance Management:**

Integrate values into performance metrics and evaluations. Align individual and team goals with the company's core values to reinforce their significance.

- **Decision-Making Framework:**

Use the values as a framework for decision-making at all levels of the organization. This ensures consistency and alignment with the company's cultural principles.

5. **Foster Open Communication:**

- **Feedback Mechanisms:**

Establish feedback mechanisms for employees to express their thoughts on the company culture and values. Act on constructive feedback to continually refine and enhance the culture.

- Transparent Communication:

Foster transparent communication regarding company decisions, changes, and plans. Openness builds trust and reinforces the commitment to the established values.

6. Encourage Collaboration and Team Building:

- Team-Building Activities:

Organize team-building activities that promote collaboration and reinforce the values. These activities can be both professional and social, fostering strong interpersonal relationships.

- Cross-Functional Collaboration:

Encourage collaboration across different departments and teams. Break down silos to create a cohesive organizational culture.

7. Provide Opportunities for Employee Development:

- Training Programs:

Implement training programs that align with the company's values. These programs can include leadership development, diversity and inclusion training, and ongoing skills enhancement.

- Mentorship and Coaching:

Offer mentorship and coaching programs to provide employees with guidance and support in their professional and personal development.

8. Celebrate Successes and Milestones:

- Recognition Programs:

Establish recognition programs to celebrate individual and team achievements that embody the company values. Publicly acknowledge and reward exemplary contributions.

- Anniversary Celebrations:

Celebrate company anniversaries and milestones. Use these occasions to reflect on the journey, reiterate values, and reinforce the shared sense of purpose.

9. **Adaptability and Evolution:**

- Periodic Assessment:

Periodically assess the effectiveness of the company culture and values. Gather feedback from employees and stakeholders to identify areas for improvement and evolution.

- Adapt to Changes:

Be adaptable to changes in the business environment and industry trends. Ensure that the company culture remains relevant and resilient in the face of evolving challenges.

10. **Embed Values in Organizational Rituals:**

- Meetings and Events:

Infuse the company values into regular meetings and special events. Use these opportunities to reinforce the cultural principles and foster a sense of belonging.

- Traditions and Ceremonies:

Establish traditions and ceremonies that embody the values. These rituals create a sense of continuity and shared identity.

11. Seek Professional Guidance:

- Culture Consultants:

Consider engaging culture consultants or experts who can provide insights and guidance on building and maintaining a positive company culture.

- Employee Surveys:

Conduct anonymous employee surveys to gauge the perception of the company culture. Use the feedback to make informed decisions about culture improvement initiatives.

12. Measure and Monitor:

- Key Performance Indicators (KPIs):

Develop KPIs related to the company culture and values. Monitor these metrics to assess the impact of cultural initiatives and identify areas for improvement.

- Regular Assessments:

Conduct regular assessments to measure the alignment of employee behaviors and attitudes with the established values. Adjust strategies based on assessment outcomes.

Establishing a strong company culture and values is an ongoing and dynamic process that requires commitment, consistency, and adaptability. By carefully defining values, communicating them effectively, and integrating them into various aspects of the organization, you create a foundation for a positive and enduring company culture that fosters success and employee satisfaction.

CHAPTER 4: SCALING STRATEGIES FOR SUSTAINABLE GROWTH

Welcome to the transformative chapter of "The Entrepreneur's Playbook" where we delve into the dynamic realm of "Scaling Strategies for Sustainable Growth." In the exhilarating journey of entrepreneurship, success isn't solely about launching a venture—it's about navigating the intricacies of growth, expansion, and long-term sustainability. This chapter serves as your guide through the strategic landscape of scaling, offering insights, methodologies, and actionable strategies that propel your business towards enduring success.

Scaling a business isn't merely a matter of increasing revenue; it's about building a robust framework that can withstand the challenges of expansion while maintaining the core values and principles that define your enterprise. Whether you're a startup aiming for accelerated growth or an established business seeking new horizons, the strategies explored in this chapter are designed to empower you with the tools needed to scale intelligently, sustainably, and in alignment with your unique vision.

We will explore the intricacies of strategic planning, operational efficiency, and resource optimization to ensure that your scaling journey is not only ambitious but also resilient. From leveraging technology and talent to exploring new markets and refining customer experiences, the scaling strategies outlined here are crafted to navigate the complexities of growth while preserving the essence of what makes your business exceptional.

As we embark on the exploration of "Scaling Strategies for Sustainable Growth," envision this chapter as your compass, guiding you through the uncharted territories of expansion with confidence and purpose. Together, let's uncover the pathways to not just growth but to enduring success, creating a legacy that stands the test of time in the ever-evolving landscape of entrepreneurship. Get ready to scale new heights and witness your entrepreneurial dreams unfold into a reality of sustained and thriving growth.

- Identifying opportunities for expansion

Identifying expansion opportunities is a crucial step in the growth and development of a business. This process involves strategic analysis, market research, and a deep understanding of the industry landscape. Here's a comprehensive guide to help identify expansion opportunities:

1. **SWOT Analysis:**

- **Strengths:**

Identify the strengths of your current business model, including unique selling points, strong customer relationships, and internal capabilities.

- **Weaknesses:**

Evaluate existing weaknesses and areas that may hinder expansion. Addressing internal weaknesses is crucial before pursuing new opportunities.

- **Opportunities:**

Look for external factors and emerging trends in the market that present expansion opportunities. Consider technological advancements, changing consumer behaviors, or gaps in the current offerings.

- **Threats:**

Assess potential threats to your business, such as competition, economic downturns, or regulatory changes. Understanding threats helps mitigate risks during the expansion process.

2. **Market Research:**

- Target Market Analysis:

Conduct a thorough analysis of your target market. Understand customer demographics, preferences, and behaviors to identify unmet needs or areas for improvement.

- Competitor Analysis:

Analyze competitors in the target market. Identify their strengths and weaknesses, and assess market saturation to find opportunities for differentiation.

- Industry Trends:

Stay abreast of industry trends and innovations. Identify emerging technologies, changing consumer preferences, and market shifts that can be leveraged for expansion.

3. **Customer Feedback:**

- Surveys and Feedback:

Gather feedback from existing customers through surveys, interviews, or online reviews. Identify areas for improvement and uncover potential opportunities based on customer needs.

- Customer Support Data:

Analyze customer support data to identify recurring issues or requests. Addressing these pain points can lead to enhanced customer satisfaction and loyalty.

4. Technology Adoption:

- Explore Technological Solutions:

Assess how emerging technologies can be integrated into your business model. This could include adopting e-commerce platforms, utilizing data analytics, or implementing automation for operational efficiency.

- Digital Presence:

Strengthen your digital presence by exploring online sales channels, social media platforms, and digital marketing strategies. This can open up new avenues for reaching a broader audience.

5. **Geographic Expansion**:

- Evaluate New Markets:

Explore the possibility of expanding into new geographic markets. Consider cultural differences, regulatory environments, and local demand for your products or services.

- International Expansion:

Assess the feasibility of international expansion. Understand the regulatory requirements, market dynamics, and cultural nuances of target countries.

6. **Diversification:**

- Product Diversification:

Explore opportunities for expanding your product or service offerings. This could involve introducing complementary products, variations, or entirely new lines to cater to a broader customer base.

- Vertical Integration:

Consider vertical integration by expanding into upstream or downstream activities within your industry. This can enhance control over the supply chain and improve efficiency.

7. Partnerships and Collaborations:

- Strategic Alliances:

Explore strategic partnerships with other businesses. This could involve collaborations for joint ventures, co-marketing efforts, or shared resources to access new markets.

- Franchising or Licensing:

Consider franchising or licensing your business model to entrepreneurs who want to replicate your success in different locations.

8. Regulatory and Legal Considerations:

- Research Regulations:

Investigate regulatory requirements for expansion, especially in new markets. Understand legal considerations and compliance standards to avoid potential obstacles.

- Intellectual Property Protection:

Ensure that your intellectual property is protected when expanding into new markets. This includes trademarks, patents, and copyrights.

9. Financial Viability:

- Financial Analysis:

Conduct a thorough financial analysis to assess the viability of expansion opportunities. Evaluate the upfront costs, projected returns, and potential risks associated with each opportunity.

- Funding Options:

Explore funding options for expansion, including internal resources, loans, investors, or crowdfunding. Ensure that the chosen funding model aligns with your growth strategy.

10. Pilot Programs:

- Test New Initiatives:

Before a full-scale expansion, consider running pilot programs or small-scale initiatives to test the waters. Use the results to refine your approach and minimize risks.

- Iterative Approach:

Embrace an iterative approach to expansion. Learn from small-scale efforts, gather feedback, and make adjustments before committing to larger investments.

11. Risk Assessment:

- Identify and Mitigate Risks:

Conduct a risk assessment for each expansion opportunity. Identify potential challenges and develop strategies to mitigate risks, ensuring a more robust and resilient expansion process.

12. Employee Capability:

- Skill Assessment:

Evaluate the skills and capabilities of your existing team. Identify areas where additional expertise may be needed to support the expansion.

- Training and Development:

Invest in training and development programs to equip your team with the necessary skills for handling the challenges of expansion.

Identifying expansion opportunities is a strategic and multifaceted process that requires a comprehensive understanding of internal strengths and weaknesses, external market dynamics, and emerging trends. By systematically exploring these factors and leveraging insights from market research, customer feedback, and industry analysis, businesses can uncover and capitalize on opportunities that align with their growth objectives. Additionally, adopting an agile and adaptive approach allows businesses to navigate the complexities of expansion while minimizing risks and maximizing the potential for sustainable growth.

- Developing effective scaling strategies

Developing effective scaling strategies is a complex yet essential aspect of business growth. It involves careful planning, strategic decision-making, and a keen understanding of market dynamics. Here's a comprehensive guide to the process of developing effective scaling strategies:

1. Set Clear Objectives:

- Define Growth Goals:

Clearly articulate the objectives of your scaling efforts. Whether it's expanding market share, entering new markets, or diversifying product offerings, having well-defined goals provides a roadmap for your scaling strategy.

- Quantifiable Metrics:

Establish quantifiable metrics to measure the success of your scaling initiatives. This could include revenue targets, customer acquisition goals, market penetration rates, or other key performance indicators (KPIs).

2. Evaluate Market Opportunities:

- Market Analysis:

Conduct a thorough analysis of the target market(s). Identify growth opportunities, assess market demand, and understand the competitive landscape. This analysis informs decisions about where and how to scale.

- Customer Segmentation:

Segment your target audience to tailor your scaling strategy to specific customer needs and preferences. Understanding different customer segments allows for more effective market penetration.

3. Operational Efficiency:

- Streamline Processes:

Evaluate and streamline internal processes to ensure operational efficiency. Efficiency gains can help manage increased demand and reduce costs associated with scaling.

- Technology Integration:

Leverage technology to automate and optimize key business processes. Implementing scalable technology solutions can enhance productivity and support growth without proportionate increases in resources.

4. Financial Planning:

- Financial Modeling:

Develop comprehensive financial models that project the costs and revenue associated with scaling. Consider various scenarios and sensitivities to ensure financial sustainability.

- Capital Allocation:

Determine the financial resources required for scaling. Assess the availability of capital through internal funding, external investment, loans, or other financing options.

5. Talent Acquisition and Development:

- Assess Workforce Needs:

Evaluate the current workforce and assess the skills and expertise needed for scaling. Identify any talent gaps that must be filled to support growth.

- Recruitment and Training:

Develop a strategic recruitment plan to attract top talent. Additionally, invest in training and development programs to upskill existing employees and align their capabilities with the demands of expansion.

6. Customer Acquisition and Retention:

- Marketing Strategies:

Develop targeted marketing strategies to reach and acquire new customers. Consider digital marketing, social media campaigns, and other channels that align with your target audience.

- Customer Retention Programs:

Implement customer retention programs to ensure that existing customers remain engaged and loyal during periods of growth. A strong focus on customer satisfaction is crucial.

7. Scalable Technology Infrastructure:

- IT Systems and Platforms:

Invest in scalable IT systems and platforms that can accommodate increased demand. Ensure that your technology infrastructure is robust enough to support the growing needs of the business.

- E-commerce and Online Presence:

Enhance your online presence, especially if applicable to your business model. An effective e-commerce platform can facilitate scaling by reaching a broader customer base.

8. Partnerships and Alliances:

- Strategic Collaborations:

Explore strategic partnerships and alliances that can facilitate scaling. This could include collaborations with other businesses, suppliers, or distributors to expand reach and capabilities.

- Franchising or Licensing:

Consider franchising or licensing your business model to leverage the expertise of local entrepreneurs and expand into new regions without significant upfront investments.

9. Risk Management:

- Identify and Mitigate Risks:

Conduct a comprehensive risk assessment for potential challenges associated with scaling. Develop risk mitigation strategies to address issues such as supply chain disruptions, regulatory changes, or economic fluctuations.

10. Pilot Programs and Iterative Approach:

- Test and Learn:

Implement pilot programs or small-scale initiatives to test the feasibility of scaling strategies. Use the insights gained to refine and optimize the approach before full-scale implementation.

- Iterative Optimization:

Embrace an iterative approach to scaling. Continuously gather feedback, monitor performance metrics, and make adjustments to the strategy based on real-world outcomes.

11. Customer Feedback and Iterative Optimization:

- Feedback Loops:

Establish feedback loops with customers and stakeholders. Actively seek input and use customer feedback to iterate on your products, services, and overall business strategy.

12. Compliance and Regulation:

- Legal and Regulatory Considerations:

Ensure compliance with legal and regulatory requirements in target markets. This includes understanding local laws, licensing, and industry-specific regulations.

- Adaptability to Regulatory Changes:

Develop a strategy for adapting to potential regulatory changes. A proactive approach to compliance minimizes disruptions during scaling.

13. **Monitoring and Evaluation:**

- Performance Metrics:

Establish key performance indicators (KPIs) to monitor the success of scaling efforts. Regularly assess and evaluate these metrics to make data-driven decisions.

- Post-Implementation Review:

Conduct a post-implementation review to assess the effectiveness of the scaling strategy. Identify successes, challenges, and areas for improvement in preparation for future scaling initiatives.

Developing effective scaling strategies is a dynamic and multifaceted process that requires a holistic approach. By aligning operational efficiency, financial planning, talent management, and customer-centric strategies, businesses can position themselves for sustainable and successful growth. The key is to remain adaptable, responsive to market dynamics, and willing to iterate on strategies based on real-world feedback and outcomes. Successful scaling isn't just about expanding the business; it's about doing so in a way that preserves the core values and strengths that define the organization.

- Managing resources and finances during periods of growth

Managing resources and finances during periods of growth is a critical aspect of sustaining and capitalizing on the expansion of a business. Effective management ensures that the organization can handle increased demand, seize new opportunities, and maintain financial stability. Here's a comprehensive guide to the process of managing resources and finances during periods of growth:

1. Financial Planning and Forecasting:

- Develop Comprehensive Financial Models:

Create detailed financial models that project revenue, expenses, and cash flow during the growth period. Consider various scenarios and sensitivities to anticipate potential challenges.

- Cash Flow Management:

Prioritize cash flow management to ensure the organization has sufficient liquidity to cover operational expenses, debt obligations, and investments in growth initiatives.

2. Budgeting and Expense Control:

- Budget Development:

Develop a detailed budget that aligns with the goals and objectives of the growth strategy. Clearly outline expenditures related to hiring, marketing, technology upgrades, and other expansion-related activities.

- Expense Control Measures:

Implement measures to control and monitor expenses. Regularly review budgets and identify areas where costs can be optimized without compromising growth objectives.

3. Capital Allocation and Funding:

- Assess Capital Needs:

Evaluate the capital requirements for the planned growth initiatives. Determine whether internal funds, external investment, loans, or a combination of financing options is the most appropriate for the scale of growth.

- Diversify Funding Sources:

Consider diversifying funding sources to mitigate risk. Explore partnerships, venture capital, angel investors, or government grants as potential avenues for financial support.

4. Operational Efficiency:

- Process Optimization:

Optimize internal processes to enhance operational efficiency. Streamline workflows, automate repetitive tasks, and identify areas for improvement to accommodate increased demand without a proportionate increase in costs.

- Technology Integration:

Leverage technology solutions to improve efficiency in various business functions. Implement scalable systems that can support growth without requiring significant manual intervention.

5. Talent Management:

- Strategic Workforce Planning:

Develop a strategic workforce plan that aligns with growth objectives. Assess the skills and expertise needed during the expansion period and plan for talent acquisition accordingly.

- Recruitment and Onboarding:

Implement a robust recruitment and onboarding process to attract and integrate new talent seamlessly. Ensure that the team is adequately equipped to handle increased workloads.

6. **Risk Management:**

- Identify and Mitigate Risks:

Conduct a thorough risk assessment to identify potential challenges associated with growth. Develop risk mitigation strategies to address issues such as supply chain disruptions, regulatory changes, or economic fluctuations.

- Insurance Coverage:

Review and update insurance coverage to mitigate financial risks associated with business operations.

This may include coverage for liability, property, and other relevant risks.

7. Strategic Partnerships and Collaborations:

- Resource Sharing:

Explore strategic partnerships and collaborations that allow for resource sharing. This can include shared facilities, joint marketing efforts, or collaborative research and development initiatives.

- Joint Ventures:

Consider joint ventures or alliances with other businesses to pool resources and share both the risks and rewards of growth initiatives.

8. Customer and Market Focus:

- Customer Retention:

Prioritize customer retention strategies to maintain existing revenue streams. Satisfied and loyal customers can provide a stable foundation during periods of growth.

- Market Segmentation:

Focus on targeted marketing strategies that align with specific customer segments. This ensures that marketing efforts are efficient and result in a higher return on investment.

9. **Monitoring and Evaluation:**

- Performance Metrics:

Establish key performance indicators (KPIs) to monitor the success of growth initiatives. Regularly assess and evaluate these metrics to make data-driven decisions.

- Adaptability:

Stay adaptable and responsive to changes in the business environment. Continuously assess the effectiveness of strategies and make adjustments based on real-time feedback and market dynamics.

10. **Legal and Regulatory Compliance:**

- Legal Review:

Conduct a legal review to ensure compliance with relevant regulations and laws associated with business expansion. Address any legal or regulatory requirements in new markets or industries.

- Intellectual Property Protection:

Ensure that intellectual property is protected during periods of growth. This includes trademarks, patents, copyrights, and any other intellectual assets critical to the business.

Effectively managing resources and finances during periods of growth requires a holistic approach that encompasses financial planning, operational efficiency, talent management, risk mitigation, and strategic decision-making. By adopting a proactive and well-coordinated strategy, businesses can navigate growth successfully, ensuring sustainability and maximizing the value derived from expansion initiatives. Regular monitoring, adaptability, and a focus on long-term financial health are key elements in managing resources and finances effectively during periods of growth.

CHAPTER 5: MARKETING MASTERY

Welcome to the transformative chapter of "The Entrepreneur's Playbook" dedicated to "Marketing Mastery." In the dynamic world of business, marketing isn't just a facet of operations—it's the art and science of connecting with audiences, building brand resonance, and driving sustained success. In this chapter, we embark on a journey through the intricacies of strategic marketing, exploring the tools, tactics, and mindset necessary to master the ever-evolving landscape of consumer engagement.

"Marketing Mastery" is more than a collection of techniques; it's a guide to understanding the essence of marketing as a driving force behind entrepreneurial triumph. Whether you're a startup founder seeking to carve a niche in a competitive market or an established business aiming to rejuvenate your brand presence, the insights and strategies unveiled here are designed to elevate your marketing game to new heights.

We delve into the core principles of effective marketing—from crafting compelling narratives that resonate with your target audience to leveraging cutting-edge digital technologies that amplify your reach. This chapter equips you with the knowledge to navigate traditional and digital channels, allowing you to tailor your approach to the unique needs of your business.

As we unravel the layers of "Marketing Mastery," envision this chapter as your companion in deciphering consumer behavior, fine-tuning your brand messaging, and optimizing your marketing mix. Whether it's harnessing the power of social media, mastering content creation, or implementing data-driven strategies, the goal is to empower you with the skills and insights needed to create a meaningful and lasting impact in the marketplace.

Let's embark on this exploration together, unlocking the secrets of effective marketing that transcend trends and stand the test of time. Whether you're a marketing novice or a seasoned entrepreneur, "Marketing Mastery" is your gateway to elevating your brand, captivating your audience, and achieving lasting success in the ever-evolving world of business. Get ready to master the art and science of marketing, and let your entrepreneurial journey be marked by resonance, relevance, and remarkable success.

- Crafting a powerful brand identity

Crafting a powerful brand identity is a strategic process that goes beyond designing a logo or creating a catchy tagline. It involves defining the essence of your brand, shaping how it is perceived, and creating a consistent and memorable experience for your audience. Here's a comprehensive guide to the process of crafting a powerful brand identity:

1. **Define Your Brand:**

- Mission and Values:

Clearly articulate your brand's mission and values. Understand the purpose and principles that drive your business, and let these guide the development of your brand identity.

- Unique Selling Proposition (USP):

Identify your unique selling proposition—the distinctive features that set your brand apart from competitors. This could be based on quality, innovation, customer service, or other factors that resonate with your target audience.

2. **Understand Your Target Audience:**

- Consumer Research:

Conduct thorough research to understand your target audience. Analyze demographics, preferences, behaviors, and psychographics to create a brand identity that resonates with your customers.

- Competitor Analysis:

Study competitors to identify gaps and opportunities in the market. Differentiate your brand by understanding what competitors offer and where you can provide unique value.

3. Create a Distinctive Visual Identity:

- Logo Design:

Develop a distinctive and memorable logo that reflects your brand's personality. Ensure that it is versatile enough to be used across various platforms and media.

- Color Palette:

Choose a color palette that conveys the emotions and attributes you want to be associated with your brand. Consistency in color reinforces brand recognition.

- Typography:

Select fonts that align with your brand personality and are easily readable. Consistent typography contributes to a cohesive brand identity.

- Imagery and Graphics:

Develop a library of visual elements, such as images and graphics that complement your brand's aesthetic. Consistency in visual elements enhances brand recognition.

4. Craft a Compelling Brand Story:

- Narrative Development:

Develop a brand story that communicates your history, values, and vision. A compelling narrative creates an emotional connection with your audience.

- Tagline:

Craft a concise and memorable tagline that encapsulates your brand's essence. A well-crafted tagline reinforces your brand message.

5. Develop Brand Personality:

- **Brand Archetype:**

Identify the archetype that aligns with your brand personality. Whether it's a hero, explorer, creator, or other archetypes, defining your brand's personality helps in consistent communication.

- **Tone of Voice:**

Establish a consistent tone of voice for all communication. Whether it's formal, casual, humorous, or authoritative, maintain a consistent language that resonates with your audience.

6. **Create Brand Guidelines:**

- **Brand Manual:**

Compile brand guidelines that outline the rules for using your brand elements. Include specifications for logo usage, color codes, typography, and any other visual or verbal elements.

- **Consistency Enforcement:**

Ensure consistency in brand application across all touchpoints, including marketing materials, website, social media, and product packaging. Consistency builds trust and recognition.

7. Online Presence:

- Website Design:

Design a website that reflects your brand identity. Consider user experience, visual elements, and content to create a cohesive online brand experience.

- Social Media Strategy:

Implement a social media strategy that aligns with your brand personality. Consistent posting and engagement reinforce your brand identity in the digital space.

8. Customer Experience:

- Consistent Customer Service:

Ensure that your customer service reflects your brand values. Consistent and positive customer interactions contribute to a strong brand identity.

- Packaging and Presentation:

Design packaging and presentation materials that align with your brand aesthetics. The physical representation of your brand contributes to the overall brand experience.

9. Brand Evolution and Adaptation:

- Adapt to Market Changes:

Stay attuned to market trends and evolving consumer preferences. Be ready to adapt your brand identity to stay relevant while maintaining core brand values.

- Periodic Brand Audits:

Conduct periodic brand audits to assess the effectiveness of your brand identity. Gather feedback from customers and stakeholders to make informed adjustments.

10. Measuring Brand Success:

- Key Performance Indicators (KPIs):

Define KPIs to measure the success of your brand identity efforts. Metrics may include brand awareness, customer loyalty, and market share.

- Surveys and Feedback:

Use surveys and feedback mechanisms to gather insights into how your audience perceives your brand. Adjust strategies based on this feedback.

Crafting a powerful brand identity is an ongoing process that requires a deep understanding of your brand, audience, and market dynamics. By thoughtfully defining your brand elements, maintaining consistency across all touchpoints, and adapting to market changes, you can create a brand identity that not only stands out but also resonates with your target audience. The ultimate goal is to forge a lasting connection that goes beyond transactions, turning customers into brand advocates who champion your brand with loyalty and enthusiasm.

- Implementing innovative marketing strategies

Implementing innovative marketing strategies is a dynamic process that involves creativity, adaptability, and a keen understanding of your target audience. Innovative strategies can help your brand stand out in a crowded marketplace, capture attention, and drive engagement. Here's a comprehensive guide to the process of implementing innovative marketing strategies:

1. **Market Research and Trend Analysis:**

- Identify Emerging Trends:

Conduct thorough market research to identify current trends and emerging opportunities. Stay informed about industry developments, consumer behaviors, and technological advancements that can influence your marketing strategy.

- Competitor Analysis:

Analyze competitors to understand their marketing strategies. Identify gaps and areas where you can differentiate your brand through innovation.

2. Customer Insights:

- Data Analytics:

Leverage data analytics to gain insights into customer behavior. Analyze data from various touchpoints to understand preferences, purchase patterns, and engagement metrics.

- Customer Surveys and Feedback:

Gather direct feedback from customers through surveys and feedback mechanisms. Understand their needs, pain points, and expectations to tailor your innovative strategies accordingly.

3. Define Clear Objectives:

- SMART Goals:

Set specific, measurable, achievable, relevant, and time-bound (SMART) objectives for your innovative marketing initiatives. Clearly define what success looks like and how it will be measured.

- Alignment with Business Goals:

Ensure that your innovative strategies align with broader business goals. Whether it's increasing brand awareness, driving sales, or launching a new product, alignment is crucial for success.

4. Cross-Functional Collaboration:

- Collaboration across Departments:

Foster collaboration between marketing teams and other departments within the organization. Cross-functional collaboration ensures that innovative ideas are integrated seamlessly into the overall business strategy.

- External Partnerships:

Explore partnerships with external entities, such as influencers, startups, or organizations that align with your brand values. Collaborative efforts can amplify the impact of your innovative marketing initiatives.

5. Content Innovation:

- Interactive Content:

Develop interactive content that engages and involves the audience. This could include quizzes, polls, interactive videos, or augmented reality experiences.

- Storytelling:

Embrace storytelling as a powerful tool for conveying your brand message. Craft narratives that resonate emotionally with your audience and create a memorable connection.

6. Leverage Technology:

- Emerging Technologies:

Embrace emerging technologies such as artificial intelligence, virtual reality, or augmented reality to create unique and immersive marketing experiences.

- Personalization through AI:

Implement AI-driven personalization to deliver tailored content and recommendations based on individual customer preferences and behaviors.

7. **Social Media Innovation:**

- New Platforms and Features:

Explore new social media platforms and features to reach a broader audience. Stay updated on the latest trends and leverage features such as live streaming, stories, or interactive polls.

- User-Generated Content:

Encourage user-generated content by involving your audience in campaigns or challenges. User-generated content adds authenticity and builds a sense of community around your brand.

8. **Innovative Campaigns:**

- Guerrilla Marketing:

Implement guerrilla marketing tactics that surprise and captivate your audience. Unconventional and memorable campaigns can generate buzz and word-of-mouth promotion.

- Cause Marketing:

Integrate cause marketing into your strategy by aligning your brand with social or environmental causes. Consumers are increasingly drawn to brands that demonstrate a commitment to positive change.

9. Agile Marketing:

- Iterative Approach:

Adopt an iterative approach to marketing. Continuously test and analyze the performance of your innovative strategies, and be ready to make adjustments based on real-time data and feedback.

- Rapid Prototyping:

Apply principles of rapid prototyping to quickly test new ideas or campaigns on a smaller scale before scaling up. This approach allows for faster learning and adaptation.

10. Measurement and Analysis:

- Key Performance Indicators (KPIs):

Define KPIs specific to your innovative marketing initiatives. Whether it's engagement metrics, conversion rates, or brand sentiment, regularly measure and analyze performance against these indicators.

- A/B Testing:

Conduct A/B testing to compare different versions of your campaigns or content. Use the insights gained to optimize and refine your innovative strategies for better results.

11. Feedback Loops:

- Customer Feedback:

Establish feedback loops with customers to understand their reactions to your innovative marketing efforts. Use this feedback to enhance and fine-tune future strategies.

- Employee Input:

Involve employees in the feedback process. Frontline employees often have valuable insights into customer reactions and can provide feedback on the feasibility and effectiveness of innovative ideas.

12. **Budget Allocation:**

- **Flexible Budgeting:**

Allocate a portion of your marketing budget specifically for innovative initiatives. Recognize that experimentation and innovation may require a flexible budget to accommodate unexpected opportunities.

- **Cost-Benefit Analysis:**

Conduct a cost-benefit analysis to evaluate the return on investment (ROI) of your innovative marketing strategies. Assess the impact on brand perception, customer acquisition, and revenue generation.

Implementing innovative marketing strategies is an ongoing and adaptive process that requires a combination of creativity, data-driven decision-making, and a willingness to embrace new approaches. By staying attuned to market dynamics, understanding customer insights, leveraging technology, and fostering a culture of innovation, businesses can position themselves as industry leaders and continually engage their audience in meaningful ways. Successful implementation of innovative marketing strategies not only drives short-term results but also builds a brand legacy that resonates with consumers over the long term.

- Leveraging digital platforms and social media for maximum impact

Leveraging digital platforms and social media for maximum impact is a multifaceted process that requires strategic planning, content excellence, and a deep understanding of your target audience. The digital landscape offers vast opportunities for brand visibility, engagement, and conversion. Here's a comprehensive guide to the process of maximizing impact through digital platforms and social media:

1. Define Clear Objectives:

- Goal Setting:

Clearly define your objectives for leveraging digital platforms and social media. Whether it's increasing brand awareness, driving website traffic, or boosting sales, having specific and measurable goals is crucial.

- Audience Segmentation:

Identify and segment your target audience. Understanding the demographics, interests, and behaviors of your audience helps in tailoring content and strategies for maximum impact.

2. Choose the Right Platforms:

- Platform Selection:

Identify the digital platforms and social media channels that align with your target audience and business goals. Consider popular platforms such as Facebook, Instagram, Twitter, LinkedIn, and emerging platforms relevant to your industry.

- Channel-Specific Strategies:

Develop channel-specific strategies based on the strengths and features of each platform. For example, use Instagram for visually appealing content, LinkedIn for professional networking, and Twitter for real-time updates.

3. Content Creation and Curation:

- High-Quality Content:

Create high-quality, visually appealing content that aligns with your brand identity. This includes images, videos, infographics, and written content that resonates with your audience.

- Consistency:

Maintain a consistent posting schedule to keep your audience engaged. Consistency builds brand awareness and loyalty. Consider using content calendars to plan and schedule posts in advance.

4. **Engagement Strategies:**

- **Community Building:**

Foster a sense of community by engaging with your audience. Respond to comments, messages, and mentions promptly. Encourage discussions and user-generated content to enhance engagement.

- **Contests and Giveaways:**

Organize contests, giveaways, or challenges to incentivize audience participation. Such activities not only boost engagement but also expand the reach of your brand through social sharing.

5. **Influencer Collaborations:**

- **Identify Influencers:**

Identify influencers or thought leaders in your industry who align with your brand values.

Collaborate with them to reach a wider audience
and build credibility.

- Authentic Partnerships:

Ensure that influencer partnerships are authentic
and resonate with your target audience. Authenticity
is key to building trust and credibility.

6. Paid Advertising:

- Targeted Ads:

Utilize targeted advertising on platforms like
Facebook and Instagram to reach specific
demographics. Define your target audience
parameters to ensure your ads are seen by the most
relevant users.

- Budget Optimization:

Optimize your advertising budget by monitoring
the performance of different ad sets. Allocate the
budget to the most effective campaigns based on
key performance indicators (KPIs).

7. Data Analytics and Insights:

- Analytics Tools:

Use analytics tools provided by social media platforms to track the performance of your content. Analyze metrics such as reach, engagement, click-through rates, and conversions.

- Iterative Optimization:

Apply insights gained from analytics to optimize your strategies iteratively. Identify what works well and refine your approach to continuously improve impact.

8. Mobile Optimization:

- Responsive Design:

Ensure that your digital content is mobile-friendly. With a growing number of users accessing social media on mobile devices, responsive design is essential for a positive user experience.

- App Integration:

Explore opportunities to integrate your brand with mobile apps or leverage features such as Instagram Shopping to facilitate seamless mobile transactions.

9. **Video Marketing:**

- Live Streaming:

Incorporate live streaming for real-time interactions with your audience. Platforms like Instagram Live, Facebook Live, and YouTube Live provide opportunities for direct engagement.

- Short-Form Content:

Experiment with short-form videos on platforms like TikTok or Instagram Reels. Short, engaging videos can capture attention in a crowded digital environment.

10. **Ephemeral Content:**

- Stories and Fleets:

Utilize ephemeral content features such as Instagram Stories, Facebook Stories, or Twitter

Fleets. These temporary posts create a sense of urgency and encourage regular audience check-ins.

11. Chatbots and Messaging Apps:

- Customer Service Automation:

Implement chatbots to automate customer service on messaging apps. Chatbots can provide instant responses, answer frequently asked questions, and guide users through processes.

- Personalized Communication:

Use messaging apps for personalized communication with customers. Send targeted offers, updates, or recommendations based on customer preferences.

12. Cybersecurity Measures:

- Protect User Data:

Prioritize cybersecurity to protect user data and maintain trust. Implement secure authentication methods, encrypt communications, and stay compliant with data protection regulations.

- Educate Users:

Educate your audience about cybersecurity best practices. Provide tips on creating strong passwords, recognizing phishing attempts, and securing personal information.

13. **Adaptability to Algorithm Changes:**

- Stay Informed:

Stay informed about algorithm changes on social media platforms. Adapt your strategies to align with these changes and ensure continued visibility in users' feeds.

- Diversify Strategies:

Diversify your digital marketing strategies to mitigate the impact of algorithm shifts. Relying on a single approach makes your brand vulnerable to sudden changes.

Leveraging digital platforms and social media for maximum impact requires a holistic and adaptive approach. By aligning your strategies with audience preferences, embracing innovation, and staying abreast of industry trends, you can create a compelling digital presence that not only engages your audience but also drives tangible business outcomes. Continuously analyze performance

, refine strategies based on data insights, and foster meaningful connections to maximize the impact of your brand in the digital realm.

CONCLUSION

In concluding "The Entrepreneur's Playbook: How to Start, Scale, and Succeed in Business," I extend my heartfelt gratitude to every reader who embarked on this transformative journey. We've explored the dynamic landscape of entrepreneurship, delving into the intricacies of initiating, expanding, and triumphing in the realm of business.

As you close these pages, I hope you carry with you not just a collection of insights and strategies, but a resilient entrepreneurial spirit. The challenges discussed, the successes celebrated, and the lessons learned collectively form a blueprint for navigating the complexities of the business world.

Remember, entrepreneurship is not merely about starting a venture; it's a perpetual voyage of growth, adaptation, and innovation. Your ability to embrace change, cultivate resilience, and lead with a visionary mindset will be the compass guiding your journey.

May you find inspiration in the stories shared within these chapters, drawing strength from the trials faced by fellow entrepreneurs who transformed obstacles into stepping stones. As you apply the knowledge gained, seize opportunities, and overcome challenges, know that the essence of entrepreneurship lies not just in reaching the destination but in relishing the journey.

Keep in mind that success is a spectrum, and each milestone achieved, every lesson learned, contributes to the evolution of your entrepreneurial narrative. Cherish the moments of triumph, learn gracefully from setbacks, and understand that the journey towards success is a continuum of growth.

In closing, let the entrepreneurial spirit encapsulated in this playbook serve as a guiding force. Whether you're at the inception of your venture or steering an established enterprise toward new horizons, may this playbook remain a companion—a source of inspiration, wisdom, and strategic guidance.

As you step into the unpredictable yet exhilarating terrain of entrepreneurship, may you find not just success but fulfilment, purpose, and a lasting legacy? The Entrepreneur's Playbook is more than a guide; it's a testament to the indomitable spirit that propels entrepreneurs to dream, innovate, and create impact.

Here's to your entrepreneurial journey—may it be marked by resilience, continuous learning, and unparalleled success. The playbook may conclude, but your entrepreneurial odyssey is just beginning. Onward to new horizons, empowered by the playbook's wisdom, and fueled by the unwavering spirit of entrepreneurship.

www.ingramcontent.com/pod-product-compliance
Lightning Source LLC
Chambersburg PA
CBHW070130260726

48658CB00001B/353